I LEARN TO READ AND WRITE THE WAY I LEARN TO TALK

A Very First Book About Whole Language

Marlene Barron
West Side Montessori School
New York City

and

Our Children

Richard C. Owen Publishers, Inc.
Katonah, New York

Library of Congress Cataloging-in-Publication Data

Barron, Marlene.
    I learn to read and write the way I learn to talk : a very
first book about whole language / by Marlene Barron and our children.
        p.   cm.
    Includes bibliographical references (p.).
    ISBN 1-878450-07-7
    1. Language arts (Preschool)   2. Language experience approach in
education.   I. Title.
LB1140.5.L3B37 1990
372.6—dc20   90-34286
                                                       CIP

RICHARD C. OWEN PUBLISHERS, INC.
135 Katonah Avenue
Katonah, New York 10536

Printed in the United States of America

Cover design and drawing by Kate Brokaw, age four years, ten months.

A Note to the Reader

Celebrating children's early years is what this book is really about. Everyday events become wondrous adventures full of discoveries and surprises when seen through children's eyes. Sharing these unbelievably creative everyday experiences is what *all* our lives are about.

I am particularly indebted to Kurt Brokaw, whose clarity of purpose helped me "get it all together." Without his assistance I might never have completed this project.

I owe a special thanks to the children and parents at West Side Montessori School; Staten Island Montessori School; and Edgemont School, a Montessori public school in Montclair, New Jersey. To the children I owe an appreciation for what they taught me about how much children know about reading and writing, and about life. When Daniel, age three, handed his mother a note he had "written," or when Jessica, age six, began her diary, "I HD MAE BTHDAY YSDRDA I EM REDN I M RITEN" and wrote on the last page "I M LONY" (I am lonely); when Jamie, age six and one-half, wrote about her "bad tims in the haopd" (hospital), I am reminded how privileged we all are to be able to share these precious moments with them.

—MB

I LEARN TO READ AND WRITE THE WAY I LEARN TO TALK

A Very First Book About Whole Language

HEL

HELEN

Helen, 4.7, People drawing.

MECE MAUS

Emily, 4.11, "Mickey Mouse"

IMAEDATAN.

Thomas, 4.5, "I made a train."

RETL

Mary, 4.7, "Reptile"

PL SSPT K P PEL

Lee, 4.0, "Please put back pencil"

Stories, and messages and captions are being "written" by typical four-year-olds every day.

Surprised? Don't be.

In our 1990s society four-year-olds, most three-year-olds, and even some two-year-olds are beginning to read and write.

They see and recognize the signs that abound in our environment—the WALK sign at the corner, the fast-food logos in the mall, the brand names on television and all around the kitchen.

A typical three-year-old understands many signs. EXIT. PUSH. STOP. DANGER. And they know countless other words from SESAME STREET to FAX to WHO YA GONNA CALL?

They write many of these words as well.

What may be rather surprising are the *settings* in which this writing and reading occur. They take place in homes, in cars, and in supermarkets—even in classrooms. They take place in unexpected settings in classrooms: the housekeeping corner, the block area, the art area, by the fish tank, and in hallways.

Everywhere.

Eddie, 3.11

Lilyanne, 3.2, "Hello"

Jordan, 3.11

Veronica, 5.3, "I wrote in script."

Alex, 2.11, "I'm writing a story."

How do young children become beginning readers and writers?

It's a natural process. Children's first babbles are a beginning stage of talking. Children's first *scribbles*—like those on the lefthand page—are the beginning of writing. Children are putting their thoughts on paper. They make up letters, tight squiggles in assorted sizes or long strokes. It happens easily and quite naturally.

Through these first scribbles children discover that writing is much, much more than just spelling, grammar, or penmanship. Writing is expressing *ideas* and *feelings* and *information* on paper, on chalkboards.

And when they "read" their marks—their writing—back to us, they discover what reading is all about. It is making sense of print. And this sense-making process is much more than just sounding out letters in words.

That's what whole language recognizes and supports—a natural way to read and write, a natural way to become literate.

Frank, 6.6, "Blackfeet Indians and Cowboys"

Jessica, 6.0, "Mom are best and Dad are best."

Zachary, 5.10, "A Spaceship"

Mary, 4.3

Children of all ages use different kinds of "talk" to make sense of their personal experiences and stories.

Children speak their thoughts, and we respond.

They dramatize—act and talk—their ideas and feelings. That's a kind of talk. And we respond.

They "talk" through song and dance. And we do, too.

They draw. That's "talk." And they describe their drawings. And we respond.

Then they write! That's "talking" on paper. And when they read their writing, we respond.

Parents and teachers the world over have long recognized these different kinds of "talking," these different ways of learning. Many have even organized programs to enhance this natural process.

Eighty years ago in Italy Maria Montessori's four-year-old students "exploded into writing" with words and messages.

Forty years ago in New Zealand Sylvia Ashton-Warner's Maori children wrote about their experiences and feelings.

Today it's happening in many homes and in more and more classrooms. Just look at the writing in this book.

It can also happen in your home and in your children's classrooms—just as it does for *all* of New Zealand's students.

WE NED FILIPS

MRLEN

Bart, 5.10, "We need Phillips [screwdrivers] Marlene"

Jordan, 5.1, "Dear Marlene, / There is ice on the fire escape. / From Jordan"

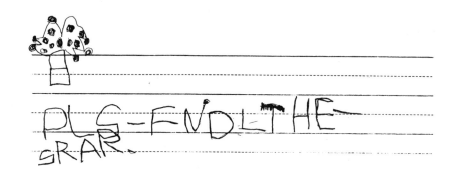

Charlie, 6.5, "Please find the strainer"

Kate, 5.7, "Dear Barry / What time will lunch be ready"

Literacy programs in New Zealand have revolutionized their way of teaching young children.

New Zealand has virtually no illiteracy. Almost every child is literate at an early age.

The key reason is that their children learn to read by reading books—nature books, history books, science books, and storybooks. They learn to write by writing. It has been a countrywide way of teaching children to read and write for decades.

It's not surprising that New Zealand's children love to write and read. Their parents and teachers have been innovators and adopters of this natural approach to literacy for a long time.

The whole language approach is gaining in popularity in England, too, and in Canada and Australia.

Here in the United States better than one in ten schools have adopted whole language. Teachers have been open to experimentation, to change, to putting aside workbooks and drill sheets that can smother children's learning (and don't even teach what they claim to teach).

Are your children's schools ready for whole language? Your children certainly are, as are the girls and boys in this book.

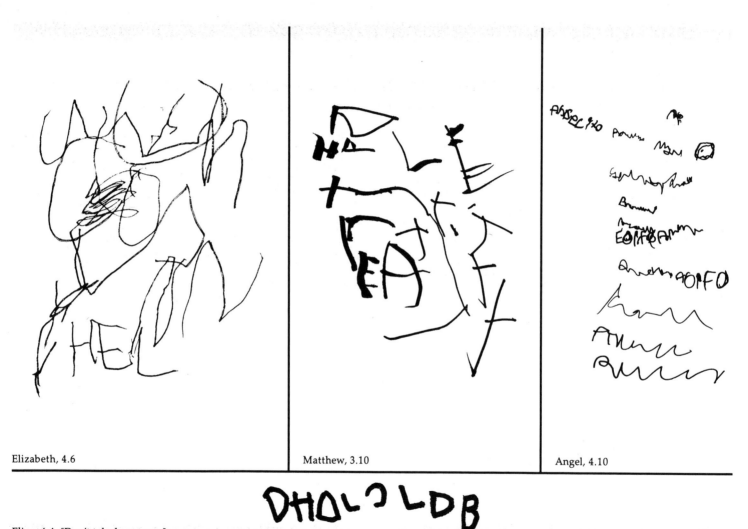

Elizabeth, 4.6

Matthew, 3.10

Angel, 4.10

Eliza, 4.4, "Don't take long turns"

What is whole language?

Whole language is a way of looking at children and how they learn. It is an attitude, a set of beliefs about how children learn. Its principles and practices are firmly grounded in research from many fields: linguistics, language development, sociolinguistics, anthropology, psychology, and education. Whole language was *not* born of economic or political or "expedient" decisions on how to educate children, as so many of the curriculum directives of state legislatures have been.

What's more, whole language is a fulltime program. It can't be done just a few hours a day. It's being with children in a way that flows through the whole curriculum, the classroom, the home—every school day and weekends too. Whole language is a part of everyday life. It can't be stuffed in a textbook or done between taking attendance and lunch.

Whole language *isn't* a book or a reading series or a course. It's not a set of "magical" materials. It's not a skills-driven approach to reading and writing.

You won't find it on a worksheet or in a workbook or in those graded readers with their restricted vocabulary, stilted language, and fragmented learning.

J FRANK

Chicago

Mohtreql Expos

NeW York Mets

phil@delphia

phillies

Pit—sby r g hp

IRqtes

S+Lou s

i nqis scapd

Frank, 6.1

I SMALL CUP
of GARPS
I CARCR WITH
CARM CEEHS
I CUP OF APL
JEI

Jonathan, 6.3, *1 small cup of grapes / 1 cracker with cream cheese / 1 cup of apple juice

HOW
TO
PLAY
BASE
BALL

BY DAVID

David, 6.3

Why children like whole language so much.

The whole language approach builds on what each child already knows. The approach looks at *how* children become readers and writers. It makes it possible for children to read real books and write to communicate—all quite naturally.

Take a simple analogy: Remember how your child first learned to walk? She or he sat up, then stood, then "cruised," holding on to furniture . . . and finally stepped out. While all that was going on your child was being gently encouraged and applauded. No "cruiser" was scolded for tumbling or was given "training" in running.

Children learn to talk much the same way. First they hear adults talking and talking. Then they babble, and we respond. Then comes the first word, "dada" or "mama." So we celebrate and respond even more! Next children use "almost" words and "almost" phrases (chunks of meaning), then more and more "almost" words and phrases, then real words and phrases, and finally sentences. They become fluent speakers in the language and regional dialects of their families.

Children talk because they have something to say. They continue to talk because they get our responses, because they are encouraged, because their language attempts are acknowledged.

In the same way reading and writing begin long before children start school. Children write because they have something to say or because they are exploring with a pencil or crayon. They read because they want to find out what was said.

We must begin to notice these beginnings, and then encourage and applaud them. The children whose work fills this book get that recognition, encouragement, and applause every day.

No wonder they like it so much.

No wonder they read and write so naturally.

Alec, 6.1, "Battle"

ON WEDAY THE 18 1989 I WATN TO THE PET SURRD WE FATT SAM

Kate, 5.8, "On Wednesday the 18 1989 I went to the pet store We bought Sam"

ME AND DAD ISCE-ing...

Sam, 5.3, "Me and Dad skiing"

Reading and writing emerges in stages, just like talking and walking.

The path to adult literacy begins at home with children hearing spoken language. It develops as they begin talking. It continues in their pretend games (like peek-a-boo) and play with dolls or cars or blocks or superhero figures. As children compose and elaborate on their pretend scenarios, they are creating original stories. As they act out parts of stories by stepping into different characters' shoes, they are understanding the story better. They are interpreting and analyzing the storyline and characters' actions.

Soon they begin to draw and paint and "talk," using all kinds of art media and materials to express their thoughts, to interpret stories, and to understand their lives.

Their first drawings emerge into pictures we, as adults, begin to recognize and identify. Soon their artwork includes printlike marks and symbols, children's names, random letters, and then some beginning sounds of words. Then we start to see their writing include those sounds the child has *heard* and *written*.

Children are spontaneously figuring out the conventions of writing. In their own way they are inventing the rules of spelling and writing—where you put spaces between words or use upper- and lower-case letters, or how you sign a letter or address an envelope.

Over time children's different kinds of "talk" about stories and experiences becomes increasingly more sophisticated and complex. That's why whole language keeps all aspects of language—talking, listening, reading, and writing—together. It keeps language whole for whole children in their whole lives.

Whole language is holistic!

Candance, 5.5

Kelsey, 4.3

Natasha, 5.0, "Rainbows cost a lot of dollars"

Kopavi, 5.2, "The sun and the moon"

The whole language approach "follows the child" rather than having the child follow the curriculum.

Remember when you first learned to read in school?

Chances are you had to follow a prescribed curriculum. Everyone in the class used the same set of graded readers. The teacher controlled the process, and you couldn't read ahead.

Whole language is nothing like that. Sure there's a curriculum—one that supports and enhances each child's emerging abilities, whatever the stage. Teachers gently guide children as they pretend to write, or scribble a thought, or draw an idea, or share a personal experience, or read a book, or sing a made-up song, or write—all those ways of "talking" and learning.

What whole language teachers *don't* do is drill children with skills and rules and procedures. We *do* provide information when children are ready for it and in a way that makes sense to them. As we read along with a beginning reader we might give the first sound in a word or ask if that sentence makes sense to the child.

We encourage children to shape and reshape their personal knowledge by "talking" with others who then do the same thing back.

That's why it's so important to talk about, or dramatize about, or draw about, or sing about, or write about a story or an experience.

And that's why everyone is talking and learning and *actively* involved in whole language classrooms.

Learning is an endlessly fascinating, interactive, social, and academic process. A *fun* process. A meaningful process. When the child is leading the process.

PETRPAN JACK

Ben, 5.5, "Peter Pan Jack"

By Deirdre

Song

We love to play
and sing and be gay.
We hate to have no
frends. I Love my
frends Alison and
Elissa and cynthia
and Elyse thats all
she has to go.

Deirdre, 6.3, "Song"

Reading aloud *with* children is key.

Children become readers mainly by being read to. When they hear their favorite books read and reread and reread again, they are drawn into the story's imaginary world and begin to care about the characters. They broaden their horizons beyond their own experiences—when the reader and the child figure out the meaning of the story together, and when they "talk" about parts of the story together.

We used to read aloud with children only before they could read themselves. Now we read aloud with children who *can* already read. Often children read to each other, and to us. And they almost always "talk" about the story with others.

That's how they see (charts, TV guides, coupons) and hear how written language is different from spoken language. ONCE UPON A TIME . . . THE END. T'WAS THE NIGHT . . . They become comfortable with the different languages and formats used in various kinds of writing, just as children surrounded by Russian language speakers understand and speak Russian (without lessons). It works that way with any language worldwide.

Literacy grows and thrives through all kinds of "talk" about stories and books. We even talk about how books are put together. "This is the front of the book. The title is . . . The illustrator is . . ."

All kinds of "talk" can start at age two—even before. Some say it should start at birth.

WoS OPoN oti M
th AR WoSS A
Babe Clde.
ho Plad WITH A
Litol GiRL
Th et Wos
hr Best Fed
To The Clde.

Sarah, 5.10, "Once upon a time / There was a / baby kitty / who played with a / little girl / that was / her best friend / to the kitty."

There's nothing pretend about "pretend" reading.

When children hear their favorite books read and reread, they soon remember the words. Then they begin to practice reading, using the same intonations and mannerisms they've heard from the readers.

We used to call this "pretend" reading, but there's nothing pretend about it. Pretend reading empowers children to practice reading, to read.

Children also practice writing—poetry, fiction, plays, letters, lists, signs, titles, charts—in the same way they practiced talking.

What is our response to all these efforts? Encouragement! Applause! We certainly don't correct a beginning walker for not being able to run, or a beginning talker for not speaking in grammatically correct sentences. We value and celebrate what each child knows and does.

As with walking and talking, so too we should respond to writing and reading.

Melissa, 5.8, "Today / Tip-it

not today / Duck-Duck Goose / Tip it Hot potato / Find the donkey's tail / Making pies / Cooking / School."

Deirdre, 7.8, "I'm a good cat / Are you   No said / the bad cat / I'm so bad / that you can't / see it"

Giula, 4.11, "1989 LOVE / Giulia / for / Mommy"

What does it take to support these emerging literacy abilities?

Supporting these emerging abilities takes classrooms and homes rich with print and oral language, places where adults and children talk and read and write because they want to.

Literacy-rich homes and classrooms are organized partly like a children's bookstore, partly like an office, and partly like a theater. They are rich with opportunities for children to explore and make discoveries.

They include all sorts of magazines and lists and signs—SHOPPING LIST—and messages.

> eggs
> milk

REMIND ME TO . . . and books—wordless books, poetry, fiction, fairy tales, books with moving parts, catalogues, nature and science books, and magazines of all kinds.

It's just like a well-organized bookstore!

Classrooms usually have a dramatic play area with a collection of basic costumes and props, just like a theater. In homes the stage is often the living room or kitchen and the costumes are "old" clothing, hats, and jewelry, so children can act out their original stories as well as those in books.

Most homes or classrooms include places to write—a writing center or a special table—with different kinds of paper and writing tools. Sometimes we create an "office" with telephones, pads and pencils, message centers, and a typewriter. Children can fill out forms, draw pictures, make out checks, write lists, compose letters, and write stories.

Children soon become authors and even publishers. They can learn to bind their books and put on covers. Their books join the other literature on their bookshelves. These are real stories by real children.

Most importantly, children think of themselves as *authors*. The impetus to write, to read what is written, and to write longer and more complex stories is born.

It is an exquisite process of joy and wonder.

WNSAP APNATIM
THER WASSPE POLTHE
NAMSWRGIMEXANDTOM
WANDAGINNEXTOHVWENED
GINNXTOWHVEBAB
THHDEGLBABTHAWBSOHPE
WAYSCEWSEXESOLD MOM
ADEBOXAND SCTESSICAWATSOO

Jessica, 6.0, "Once upon a time / there was 2 people there / names were Ginny &
Tom / Tom wanted Ginny to have wanted / Tom Ginny to have a baby / They had
a girl baby / They were so happy / When she was 3 years old Mom / had a boy and
she Jessica went to school"

M U N H E N

Maura, 4.2, "Amphibian"

ONSE A PAN
A TIME TARE
WAS A CAT

SHE WAS SO
BIG.

THE END

Kate, 5.8, "Once upon / a time there / was a cat / She was so /
big. / The end."

Sam, 6.3, "Once there was a / television that monsters / crept
out of it"

The most important attitude in making whole language work is yours.

For whole language to work there must be an attitude that treats children and adults as active learners—a belief that they *can* learn and *want* to learn. An approach that lets them make decisions and work on activities that interest them and at their own pace is crucial.

The result is that children become life-long learners.

Parents and teachers, siblings and classmates are collaborators in this social process as they talk, read, write, dramatize, and dance together. Everyone strives to help and encourage others. Successes, even small ones, are celebrated. A feeling of mutual respect permeates the setting as everyone learns from and teaches others. A community of learners is created.

And everyone soon becomes comfortable with their mistakes, for all learning (from skiing to writing to talking to reading to roller skating) involves risk-taking, on-going evaluation, and new attempts. And throughout this learning process each child must lead his or her own progress.

The adult's careful planning and commitment to successful learning experiences for each child must be present. When it is, you feel it, you sense it, and *you see the results throughout the curriculum.* For in whole language classrooms children also "talk" to explore ideas and problem-solve in science, math, social studies, history—in all content areas. That's why whole language teachers love teaching. Those workbooks and ditto sheets are gone forever; and they won't be missed by either the teachers or the children!

SAM

TISEIS THE MAN PLAINe
*THE BASFII DI

Sam, 6.5, "This is the man playing the bass fiddle"

DR DADDY

U RNOUT SGKLAS

BRFRKST

8:15

Rebecca, 4.5, "Dear Daddy / You are invited to our class / breakfast / 8:15"

Jordan, 4.9, "3 people"

PEPI

This natural approach to literacy can work in every language worldwide.

Of all the things in today's world that are branded "world class" whole language certainly deserves this phrase.

For a three-year-old in Kyoto has the same literary potential as a three-year-old in Capetown, Quebec, or Kansas City. The scribbles and letters and sentences of a Saudi Arabian child parallel those of a Chinese or a Bengali or an American child.

It seems that the "window of opportunity" is open for these years just about everywhere.

Three-year-olds and five-year-olds and seven-year-olds must be given the freedom, the opportunity, the right to take risks, to explore, to make discoveries, to make errors, to score victories, to achieve breakthroughs.

Whole language empowers children as it empowers teachers as it empowers parents.

The risks are small. The rewards are real. You're seeing just a few of them in the illustrations in this book.

This is my brother I love my
brother we get along pretty
well. Most of the time we
have lots of fun but some
times we fite.
My brother is it

Shannon, 6.8, "My Brother / This is my brother. I love my / brother. We get along pretty / well. Most of the time we / have lots of fun but some / times we fight. My brother is it."

Ryan, 6.0, "Ryan wins / Motorcycles / He smashed / Ryan and / Chip are winners / Chip smashes"

Frank, 6.3, "War began in the Southern States."

Whole language is the leading-edge path to literacy in the 90s and beyond.

Educating children to be literate in the twenty-first century is no easy task. It demands the best of whatever *best* unifies listening, talking, reading, writing, and thinking.

With whole language, teachers and parents are partners—real collaborators—with children in their process of becoming literate.

That's why so many key national professional groups support whole language.

But there's another group behind the process whose "work" and "experience" may be the most important of all: the children whose work fills this book.

It's their writing, their dreams, their learning.

Make it yours.

Tomorrow isn't too early to start.

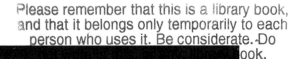

Professional Organizations You Might Contact

Whole Language Umbrella
Dorothy Watson, President
Department of Curriculum & Instruction
University of Missouri
225 Townsend Hall
Columbia, MO 65211

The National Writing Project
University of California
School of Education
5627 Tolmen Hall
Berkeley, CA 94720

American Montessori Society
150 Fifth Avenue
New York, New York 10011

Books You Might Enjoy Reading

Ashton-Warner, S. (1963). *Teacher.* N.Y.: Simon and Schuster. The personal story of a gifted teacher's approach to teaching based on joy and love.

Bird, L. B. (1989). *Becoming a Whole Language School: The Fair Oaks Story.* Katonah, N.Y.: Richard C. Owen Publishers. The struggles and successes of one school using whole language.

Butler, D., and M. Clay. (1987). *Reading Begins at Home: Preparing Children for Reading before They Go to School.* Portsmouth, N.H.: Heinemann. Practical suggestions on how parents can help children become "real" readers.

Clay, M. (1987). *Writing Begins at Home: Preparing Children for Writing before They Go to School.* Portsmouth, N.H.: Heinemann. Colorful examples of children's writing as they discover "secrets of printed language."

Cochrane, O., D. Cochrane, S. Scalena, and E. Buchanan. (1984). *Reading, Writing and Caring.* Katonah, N.Y.: Richard C. Owen Publishers. Whole language classroom strategies at various stages of reading development. A must for teachers!